CW01262078

FRANCIS FRITH'S

AROUND ABERGAVENNY

PHOTOGRAPHIC MEMORIES

RICHARD DAVIES taught in secondary schools in Coventry, Long Eaton, Bassaleg and Abergavenny. At the time of his retirement he was Deputy Headteacher at King Henry VIII School in Abergavenny. He has been the Chairman of Abergavenny Local History Society since 2000 and has written books about the history of the area, where he has lived since 1985. His other interests include choral singing, hill walking and family history. He lives with his wife, Carolyn, in the village of Pandy, six miles from Abergavenny.

FRANCIS FRITH'S
PHOTOGRAPHIC MEMORIES

AROUND ABERGAVENNY

PHOTOGRAPHIC MEMORIES

RICHARD DAVIES

First published in the United Kingdom in 2004 by
Frith Book Company Ltd

Limited Hardback Subscribers Edition Published in 2004
ISBN 1-85937-843-9

Paperback Edition 2004
ISBN 1-85937-844-7

Text and Design copyright © Frith Book Company Ltd
Photographs copyright © The Francis Frith Collection

The Frith photographs and the Frith logo are reproduced under
licence from Heritage Photographic Resources Ltd, the owners of
the Frith archive and trademarks

All rights reserved. No photograph in this publication may be sold
to a third party other than in the original form of this publication,
or framed for sale to a third party. No parts of this publication may
be reproduced, stored in a retrieval system, or transmitted, in any
form, or by any means, electronic, mechanical, photocopying,
recording or otherwise, without the prior permission of the
publishers and copyright holder.

British Library Cataloguing in Publication Data

Francis Frith's Around Abergavenny - Photographic Memories
Richard Davies

Frith Book Company Ltd
Frith's Barn, Teffont,
Salisbury, Wiltshire SP3 5QP
Tel: +44 (0) 1722 716 376
Email: info@francisfrith.co.uk
www.francisfrith.co.uk

Printed and bound in Great Britain

Front Cover: **ABERGAVENNY**, *Cross Street 1914* 67667
Frontispiece: **ABERGAVENNY**, *Sugar Loaf and Rholben from the River c1960* A9084

*The colour-tinting is for illustrative purposes only, and is not intended
to be historically accurate*

AS WITH ANY HISTORICAL DATABASE THE FRITH ARCHIVE IS CONSTANTLY
BEING CORRECTED AND IMPROVED AND THE PUBLISHERS WOULD WELCOME
INFORMATION ON OMISSIONS OR INACCURACIES

CONTENTS

FRANCIS FRITH: VICTORIAN PIONEER	7
ABERGAVENNY - AN INTRODUCTION	10
AROUND ABERGAVENNY	15
INDEX AND ACKNOWLEDGEMENTS	89
FURTHER READING	90
NAMES OF SUBSCRIBERS	91
Free Mounted Print Voucher	93

FRANCIS FRITH
VICTORIAN PIONEER

FRANCIS FRITH, founder of the world-famous photographic archive, was a complex and multi-talented man. A devout Quaker and a highly successful Victorian businessman, he was philosophical by nature and pioneering in outlook.

By 1855 he had already established a wholesale grocery business in Liverpool, and sold it for the astonishing sum of £200,000, which is the equivalent today of over £15,000,000. Now a very rich man, he was able to indulge his passion for travel. As a child he had pored over travel books written by early explorers, and his fancy and imagination had been stirred by family holidays to the sublime mountain regions of Wales and Scotland. 'What lands of spirit-stirring and enriching scenes and places!' he had written. He was to return to these scenes of grandeur in later years to 'recapture the thousands of vivid and tender memories', but with a different purpose. Now in his thirties, and captivated by the new science of photography, Frith set out on a series of pioneering journeys up the Nile and to the Near East that occupied him from 1856 until 1860.

INTRIGUE AND EXPLORATION

These far-flung journeys were packed with intrigue and adventure. In his life story, written when he was sixty-three, Frith tells of being held captive by bandits, and of fighting 'an awful midnight battle to the very point of surrender with a deadly pack of hungry, wild dogs'. Wearing flowing Arab costume, Frith arrived at Akaba by camel sixty years before Lawrence of Arabia, where he encountered 'desert princes and rival sheikhs, blazing with jewel-hilted swords'.

He was the first photographer to venture beyond the sixth cataract of the Nile. Africa was still the mysterious 'Dark Continent', and Stanley and Livingstone's historic meeting was a decade into the future. The conditions for picture taking confound belief. He laboured for hours in his wicker dark-room in the sweltering heat of the desert, while the volatile chemicals fizzed dangerously in their trays. Back in London he exhibited his photographs and was 'rapturously cheered' by members of the Royal Society. His reputation as a photographer was made overnight.

VENTURE OF A LIFE-TIME

Characteristically, Frith quickly spotted the opportunity to create a new business as a specialist publisher of photographs. He lived in an era of immense and sometimes violent change.

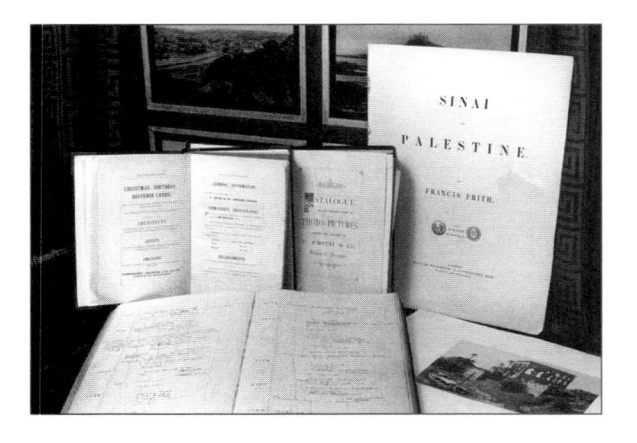

For the poor in the early part of Victoria's reign work was exhausting and the hours long, and people had precious little free time to enjoy themselves. Most had no transport other than a cart or gig at their disposal, and rarely travelled far beyond the boundaries of their own town or village. However, by the 1870s the railways had threaded their way across the country, and Bank Holidays and half-day Saturdays had been made obligatory by Act of Parliament. All of a sudden the working man and his family were able to enjoy days out and see a little more of the world.

With typical business acumen, Francis Frith foresaw that these new tourists would enjoy having souvenirs to commemorate their days out. In 1860 he married Mary Ann Rosling and set out on a new career: his aim was to photograph every city, town and village in Britain. For the next thirty years he travelled the country by train and by pony and trap, producing fine photographs of seaside resorts and beauty spots that were keenly bought by millions of Victorians. These prints were painstakingly pasted into family albums and pored over during the dark nights of winter, rekindling precious memories of summer excursions.

THE RISE OF FRITH & CO

Frith's studio was soon supplying retail shops all over the country. To meet the demand he gathered about him a small team of photographers, and published the work of independent artist-photographers of the calibre of Roger Fenton and Francis Bedford. In order to gain some understanding of the scale of Frith's business one only has to look at the catalogue issued by Frith & Co in 1886: it runs to some 670 pages, listing not only many thousands of views of the British Isles but also many photographs of most European countries, and China, Japan, the USA and Canada - note the sample page shown on page 9 from the hand-written Frith & Co ledgers recording the pictures. By 1890 Frith had created the greatest specialist photographic publishing company in the world, with over 2,000 sales outlets - more than the combined number that Boots and WH Smith have today! The picture on the next page shows the Frith & Co display board at Ingleton in the Yorkshire Dales (left of window). Beautifully constructed with a mahogany frame and gilt inserts, it could display up to a dozen local scenes.

POSTCARD BONANZA

The ever-popular holiday postcard we know today took many years to develop. In 1870 the Post Office issued the first plain cards, with a pre-printed stamp on one face. In 1894 they allowed other publishers' cards to be sent through the mail with an attached adhesive halfpenny stamp. Demand grew rapidly, and in 1895 a new size of postcard was permitted called the court card, but there was little room for illustration. In 1899, a year after Frith's death, a new card measuring 5.5 x 3.5 inches became the standard format, but it was not until 1902 that the divided back came into being, so that the address and message could be on one face and a full-size illustration on the other. Frith & Co were in the vanguard of postcard development: Frith's sons Eustace and Cyril continued their father's monumental task, expanding the number of views offered to the public and recording more and more places in Britain, as the coasts and countryside were opened up to mass travel.

Francis Frith had died in 1898 at his villa in Cannes, his great project still growing. The archive he created continued in business for another seventy years. By 1970 it contained over a third of a million pictures showing 7,000 British towns and villages.

FRANCIS FRITH'S LEGACY

Frith's legacy to us today is of immense significance and value, for the magnificent archive of evocative photographs he created provides a unique record of change in the cities, towns and villages throughout Britain over a century and more. Frith and his fellow studio photographers revisited locations many times down the years to update their views, compiling for us an enthralling and colourful pageant of British life and character.

We are fortunate that Frith was dedicated to recording the minutiae of everyday life. For it is this sheer wealth of visual data, the painstaking chronicle of changes in dress, transport, street layouts, buildings, housing, engineering and landscape that captivates us so much today. His remarkable images offer us a powerful link with the past and with the lives of our ancestors.

THE VALUE OF THE ARCHIVE TODAY

Computers have now made it possible for Frith's many thousands of images to be accessed almost instantly. Frith's images are increasingly used as visual resources, by social historians, by researchers into genealogy and ancestry, by architects and town planners, and by teachers involved in local history projects.

In addition, the archive offers every one of us an opportunity to examine the places where we and our families have lived and worked down the years. Highly successful in Frith's own era, the archive is now, a century and more on, entering a new phase of popularity. Historians consider the Francis Frith Collection to be of prime national importance. It is the only archive of its kind remaining in private ownership. Francis Frith's archive is now housed in an historic timber barn in the beautiful village of Teffont in Wiltshire. Its founder would not recognize the archive office as it is today. In place of the many thousands of dusty boxes containing glass plate negatives and an all-pervading odour of photographic chemicals, there are now ranks of computer screens. He would be amazed to watch his images travelling round the world at unimaginable speeds through internet lines.

The archive's future is both bright and exciting. Francis Frith, with his unshakeable belief in making photographs available to the greatest number of people, would undoubtedly approve of what is being done today with his lifetime's work. His photographs depicting our shared past are now bringing pleasure and enlightenment to millions around the world a century and more after his death.

ABERGAVENNY
AN INTRODUCTION

ABERGAVENNY is a busy border market town of some antiquity with a mixture of ancient and modern buildings. Long known as the 'Gateway to Wales', it is a few miles from the English border; it opens the way to rural Monmouthshire and Powys, to the industrial valleys of the south, and to the many mountain ranges of Wales.

It is the setting of the town that makes an immediate impact. The area is one of outstanding natural beauty, of lush meadows in river valleys set among surrounding hills. The three largest of its seven hills are the Blorenge, Skirrid Fawr, and the Sugar Loaf. None of the three is more than 2000 feet high, but their individually distinctive shapes render them instantly memorable. The town itself is at the junction of the small Gavenny stream, which gives the town its name, and the river Usk. The Usk, beginning near Trecastle in rural Breconshire, wends its ever widening course through Brecon and

ABERGAVENNY, *The River Usk and the Sugar Loaf 1898* 41672

Crickhowell to Abergavenny before continuing its journey to the Severn below Newport.

Human settlement in the area began some 14,000 years ago, and early activities included hunting, fishing and fighting, as the surviving prehistoric tools and weapons in the town's Castle Museum show. The many Iron Age hillforts in the area include Table Mountain or Crug Hywel at Crickhowell and those on the southern edges of the Black Mountains at Twyn-y-Gaer and Pentwyn. These were the scenes of tribal warfare, and it was the successful Silures tribe which presented the Romans with their greatest challenge when they arrived in the first century AD. To the Romans, Abergavenny was Gobannium, a place of iron workers. Unfortunately, the site of the Roman fort built between AD 55 and AD 57 is now covered by the Castle Street car park, but at least the archaeologists had time to excavate the site, and their finds are in the museum a few hundred yards away.

The Normans, who called the town Burgavenny, have left more visible evidence of their presence, not least in the ruins of the castle and in the Priory Church of St Mary. To see the reasons for their settlement it is only necessary to stand on the raised outcrop of land on which the Romans and the Normans built their fortresses. From the top of the Norman motte the approach of an enemy force would have been quickly spotted.

The Norman marcher lord credited with the construction of the castle and the priory at the end of the 11th century is Hamelin de Ballon, a leading supporter of William the Conqueror. He, like many other marcher lords who were given land in the Marches (or border country), assumed a considerable degree of independence. The castle was a visible symbol of the power he meant to retain, whilst the Benedictine monks and their prior, who came over from near Le Mans in Normandy, legitimised that power.

The local Welsh lords inevitably came into conflict with the military might and pretensions of the marcher lords. Their differences led to the most infamous event in Abergavenny's history. At Christmas 1175 the Norman lord, William de Braose, invited Seisyll ap Dyfnwal and other Welsh lords to a banquet in the hall of the castle, where his men massacred them. Seisyll had earlier murdered William's uncle: predictably, further Welsh reprisals followed.

The Norman walled town had entrance gates on four sides, and for centuries virtually all of the town was enclosed inside these walls. Records of the town's defences survive in the form of murage grants made in the 13th and early 14th centuries. These allowed the town to levy taxes or tolls to pay for town fortifications (yet the town was soon to face major new threats). In the late 1340s it was ravaged by the Black Death, and the sharp fall in population which that entailed was to lead to a big reduction in rents from surrounding hamlets like Llanover. Fifty years later, like many other towns in Wales, Abergavenny was attacked by the followers of Owain Glyndwr during his rebellion against the English king. Parts of St Mary's and the tithe barn were burned at this time.

The parish church of the town was St John's, but members of the ruling families of Abergavenny, such as the Hastings, were buried in the Priory Church of St Mary. Long before the Reformation, the priory itself was in decline both in standards and in the number of monks. With the dissolution of the monasteries, when the priory was closed, the tithes which had paid for its upkeep were used in 1542 to finance the town's King Henry VIII Grammar School for Boys at St John's. Increasingly St Mary's, just outside the town walls, was the church for the people of the town, and now it succeeded St John's as the parish church.

For all the importance of the castle and church, the heart of the town was to be found in the street markets held near St John's from early Norman times. Animals and produce were sold here, as we can see from the surrounding street-names like Chicken Street and Flannel Street. When Leland visited the town between 1535 and 1543, he referred to it as 'a faire waulled town, meately well inhabited'. To George Owen, writing in 1602, it was 'a fine town, wealthy and thriving, and the very best in the shire'. By the 17th century, the market had moved to the top of Cross Street, where a market house had been built. Later, in 1796, a new courtyard market designed by John Nash was opened. By the early 19th century, Abergavenny had begun to expand beyond its town walls. In 1863 a new site was found for the livestock market; the mart still stands there, though its future is being debated.

As a market town with a large agricultural hinterland, Abergavenny's main industry for centuries was agriculture, but there were also many associated trades. A tannery flourished at the junction of Mill Street and Lower Cross Street from the 17th to the early 19th centuries. Other industries linked to it made gloves, boots and shoes, and saddles and harnesses. There is only one saddler left today, and the boot and shoe industry has relocated to the Midlands. The flannel making industry also enjoyed a period of prosperity, with several small weaving factories being set up in the town and area in the 17th and early 18th centuries. Goats provided the hair which made periwigs in the 18th century. The hair of goats was valued in proportion to its whiteness, and it sold well. A method of bleaching was said to have been invented in Abergavenny, but by the early 19th century periwigs too had gone out of fashion.

The character of the town has also been shaped by the industrial communities which developed on the slopes of the Blorenge. Iron making came early to Llanelly Hill and

ABERGAVENNY, *Cross Street 1898* 41675

Blaenavon, and coal mining also transformed the appearance of the valleys of North Monmouthshire. Brynmawr, high in the hills, had coal and iron works too, but like Blaenavon it suffered in the inter-war recession years. Brynmawr's spirit was shown by its own community-based co-operative schemes, and their story is well told in the town's new museum. Blaenavon's hopes of regeneration are founded on the Big Pit Mining Museum and a recently-launched attempt to become a book town like Hay-on-Wye. Most significantly, the Blaenavon Industrial Landscape achieved World Heritage status in 2000. In their hey-day, the industrial areas north of the Blorenge attracted workers from far and wide, and their towns became wealthy. Economic conditions defined the relationship between Abergavenny and these industrial settlements. In good times, wealthy industrialists bought large properties in Abergavenny. It would be easy to categorise Abergavenny as part of a rich pastoral lowland, insulated from the smoky industrial areas and a refuge from them. Yet this would be a misleading picture. Commercial and economic factors meant that the industrial areas forged ever closer links with Abergavenny. In times of economic downturn, the Abergavenny Poor Law Union found that the burden of the poor rate escalated alarmingly, as for many years this Union included many of the industrial districts too. Transport brought the areas together as well. Successively tramways, canals and railways were built to transport goods and—in the case of the railways—passengers.

The tramways have long gone, but the Monmouth & Brecknock canal has developed a new lease of life as a base for leisure craft and for thriving boat hire companies. On its way from Brecon to Pontymoile, it passes through rural Powys and Gwent. At Llangattock it enjoys views across the Usk valley to Crickhowell and then skirts Abergavenny, passing through Gilwern, Govilon and Llanfoist before turning south on the outskirts of Llanellen and Llanover. At one stage, Abergavenny had three railway stations: the town station, off the Monmouth Road, which remains open today, and the Junction and Brecon Road stations which have now closed.

There is a Welsh dimension to Abergavenny. Welsh is not the main language, but a cursory look at the map will reveal many Welsh place-names in the area and even in Herefordshire. There is widespread interest in learning the language, and a growing awareness of the Welsh traditions of the area with the revival of the town's eisteddfod. It is curious that it was a remarkable English woman, Augusta Waddington (she became Lady Llanover), who was a leading supporter of the town's Welsh Society, Cymreigyddion Y Fenni, founded in 1833. It held a series of eisteddfodau between 1834 and 1853, which drew huge crowds to the town. Augusta campaigned for a Welsh education, revived the use of the harp and many of the old folk songs of Wales, produced Welsh cloth, and encouraged a national costume. Today there are thriving Welsh medium schools in Abergavenny and other parts of Monmouthshire. The county is now regarded as part of Wales in a way that it was not from the days of the Tudor Act of Union onwards, when Wales was often referred to as 'Wales and Monmouthshire'.

There is a determination not to repeat the errors made by planners in the 1950s and 60s when the heart of the town centre was demolished. Old buildings such as those in Castle Street, St John's Square, Tudor Street and Mill Street were pulled down and either not replaced at all, or replaced by inferior modern buildings like the present post office. In 2003 Monmouthshire County Council decided that the town's mart should close. When it leaves the town, major decisions will have to be made about the re-development of such a large site. Plans are also in hand to re-develop the brewery yard part of the market site. Today there is a heightened awareness of development issues; let us hope that these changes will be forward-looking, whilst at the same time safeguarding the town's character. The commendable work of the St Mary's Development Trust has led to the restoration of the church's monuments. Those in the Herbert chapel in particular have revived an interest in the Herbert family, who were responsible for the great days of Raglan Castle from the 15th to the 17th centuries. A new Priory Centre has also been built, and the tithe barn has been restored imaginatively. The labour of love that is the Abergavenny Tapestry project promises to draw even more visitors to the town.

The long artery of town centre shopping from Lower Cross Street through to Frogmore Street remains, with the busy markets still the focus of Abergavenny's activities. On Tuesdays and Fridays, market days, the town overflows with farmers from miles around, shoppers from the rural areas and the industrial valleys, salesmen, day trippers and others. The Market Hall is also the venue for the weekly flea market, regular farmers' markets, and craft fairs. The Summer Festival, the highly regarded Food Festival and the Christmas Festival, all held annually, have added to the town's attractions.

Such events attract an incredibly rich mixture of people and accents to Abergavenny. The town and its comprehensive school, King Henry VIII School, have forged links with towns in France, Germany, Italy and Spain, and there are frequent foreign visits. Such a rich racial and linguistic mix is entirely appropriate in this border town; Abergavenny has known a long succession of people who have come to fight, work, pray, visit or simply settle here in this beautiful place.

CRICKHOWELL, *The End of the Bridge 1931* C188004

AROUND ABERGAVENNY

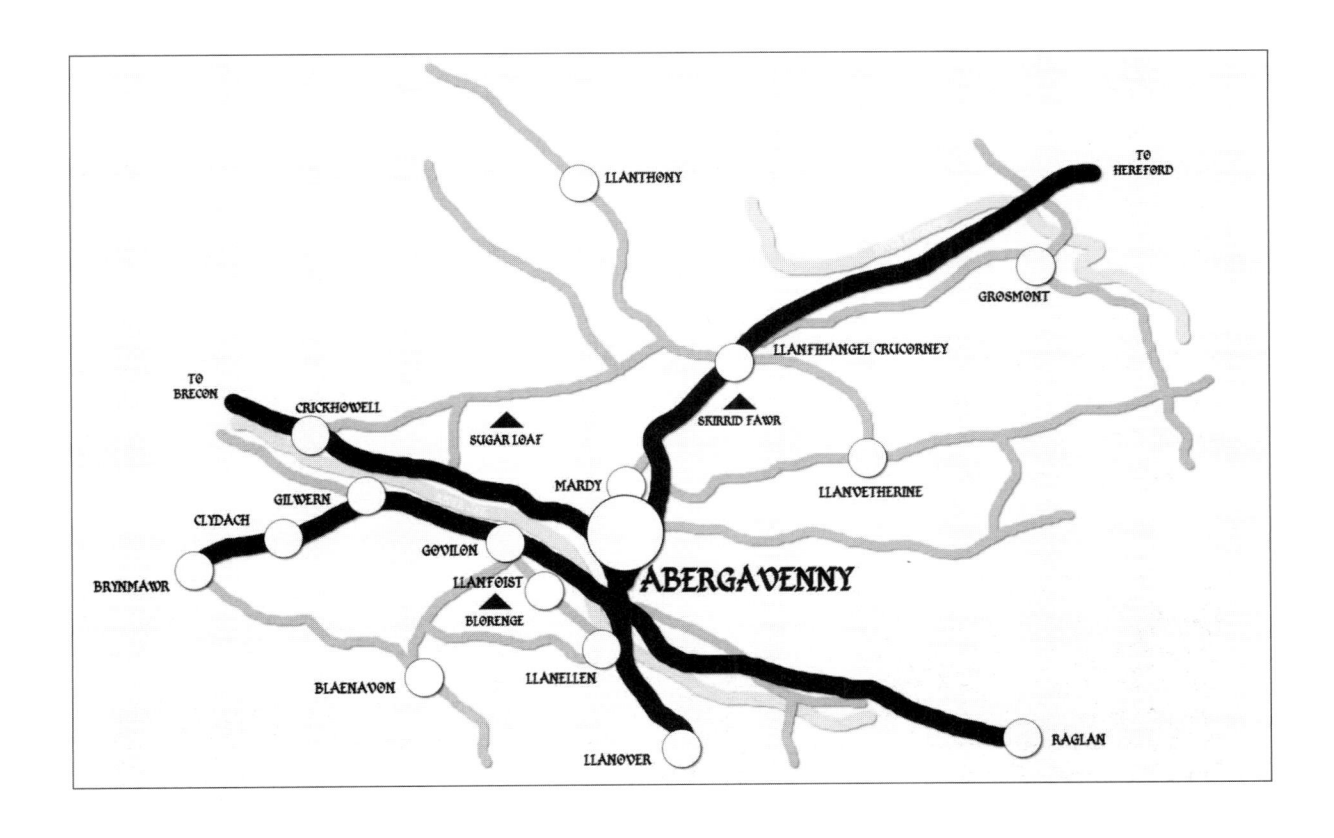

ABERGAVENNY, *Map of the Surrounding Area* ZZZ00262

FRANCIS FRITH'S - ABERGAVENNY

AROUND ABERGAVENNY

ABERGAVENNY
The Sugar Loaf c1960
A9062

The Welsh name for the Sugar Loaf is Pen Y Fal, meaning 'top of the round hill'. Whilst this 1955ft-high mountain can be climbed from Abergavenny, many of the paths that lead from its summit descend to scattered villages in remote valleys like the Grwyne Fawr and Grwyne Fechan. Often you can walk for miles in its foothills without meeting another person.

▶ **ABERGAVENNY,** *The Sugar Loaf and Rholben from the River c1960* A9084

This is a tale of two paths. A growing army of walkers now take the wide path which snakes up the Sugar Loaf to the left. A less widely used path is that below the castle walls on the right, which winds around from the main entrance to Mill Street.

◀ **ABERGAVENNY**
The Sugar Loaf from the River 1898 41668

Below the Sugar Loaf on the western outskirts of Abergavenny stands Nevill Court, previously named The Brooks. It was re-named by William Nevill, Marquess of Abergavenny, when he bought it in 1890. A previous owner, the Blaenavon industrialist James Hill, had spent a lot of money on the house. Today it is part of the modern Nevill Hall Hospital, which was built in the 1960s.

▲ **ABERGAVENNY**, *Holy Mountain 1898* 41674

In medieval times a chapel dedicated to St Michael stood on the 1595ft summit of Skirrid Fawr, Holy Mountain. Among many legends locally were that its soil had healing properties and that the cleft in its western slopes occurred at the time of the Crucifixion. It is also possible that its Welsh name, Ysgyryd, comes from ysgariad, meaning 'separation' or 'divorce'. Archdeacon Coxe, who wrote a famous account of his travels through the county in 1801, reached the summit of the Skirrid 'with animation and lassitude, horror and delight'. Certainly any worshippers at the summit chapel must have found reaching the elevated site a challenge too.

◀ **ABERGAVENNY**
The Black Mountains from Crucorney c1960
A9117

The ridge of Hatterall Hill and the Black Mountains in the distance is the route for a walk with panoramic views to Hay Bluff. This is the area of Offa's Dyke Path; it is named after the 8th-century Mercian king who built a dyke from the Severn to the Dee to shut the Welsh out. In doing so, he helped to define the borders of Wales.

FRANCIS FRITH'S - ABERGAVENNY

AROUND ABERGAVENNY

ABERGAVENNY
Below the Sugar Loaf
c1955 A9025

The symmetry of the ploughman's furrows consign the hills of Bryn Arw and the Sugar Loaf to a background role. The Pandy and Monnowside Ploughing and Agricultural Society, formed in 1867, continues to hold annual competitions in agrarian crafts like this. Seen in the centre of the photograph, but also marginalized, are the houses alongside the old Hereford Road and the steam of the Hereford to Abergavenny train.

FRANCIS FRITH'S - ABERGAVENNY

▲ ABERGAVENNY
The Blorenge 1893 32592

Two bridges crossed the Usk at Llanfoist: the medieval stone-arched road bridge is dwarfed by the railway bridge, which was demolished shortly after the Abergavenny to Merthyr line closed in the early 1960s. Behind them are the spired buildings of the new town cemetery, which was to be opened in 1894. The shadowed slopes of the Blorenge dominate the skyline. On the right, on the town side of the bridge, are the chimneys of the town's gasworks. In 1894 the Gas Committee of the Improvement Commissioners debated the introduction of electricity to supplement the gas supply, but it was 1932 before public electricity was to be added to the town's amenities.

detail of 32592

AROUND ABERGAVENNY

ABERGAVENNY
The Bridge c1965
A9138

There seems to be ample room beneath the wide arches of Llanfoist Bridge, but when the Usk floods the waters have often risen to the top of them and flooded the Castle Meadows in the foreground.

ABERGAVENNY, *The River Usk and Blorenge Mountain c1955* A9044
The home-made stile in the foreground has a temporary air. The electricity pylon beyond it is less elegant but more permanent, and remains a familiar sight today. Abergavenny had debated the merits of public electricity for nearly 40 years before it was finally introduced - only for it to be affected by the wartime blackout. The house across the river is Pen-y-worlod.

23

FRANCIS FRITH'S - ABERGAVENNY

◀ **ABERGAVENNY**
From the Blorenge
c1960 A9122

The church, castle and market hall, the historic heart of the town, remain at the centre, but more modern housing fans out from it in this scene. The landmark factory building on the left, occupied by Coopers Filters for years, was demolished in 2003–2004.

AROUND ABERGAVENNY

◀ **ABERGAVENNY**
The View towards Abergavenny 1898
41669

To a current inhabitant, the most striking feature of this view is the absence of houses in the centre. The development of Park Crescent, Croesonnen Park and the large estates beneath the Deri had yet to take place.

▲ **ABERGAVENNY,** *The View from the Blorenge c1965* A9133

The view from the 1833ft summit of the Blorenge is one of the most spectacular in Wales; but the road that crosses the mountain from Blaenavon to Govilon and Llanfoist is fairly narrow and steeply sided, so drivers cannot allow their attention to wander! Early maps have the name Bloreys or 'bare spot' for the mountain - this was a name given to high exposed places.

◀ **ABERGAVENNY**
Monmouth Road 1914
67670s

Today this road has far more traffic than a solitary horse and cart. The buildings on the right stand at the junction with Belmont Road, and are now the Belmont Inn. Opposite is the long wall of one of the substantial villas of this road, Halidon House. The villas formed part of a Victorian suburb which grew up near the town's railway station, which opened in 1854.

25

FRANCIS FRITH'S - ABERGAVENNY

▲ **ABERGAVENNY,** *St Mary's Church and the Bus Depot c1950* A9051
   There is a spring in the step of the young soldiers who have just been dropped off at the bus station. The station itself is a vast open space without the approach road and the marked bays for the cars, buses and lorries of today.

AROUND ABERGAVENNY

◀ ABERGAVENNY
The Gavenny 1898
41685s

The house has now gone, and the bridge has been replaced by another. This photograph was taken in Lower Monk Street near the weir in Swan Meadows. The building may be the Priory Mill, which was owned by the Phillips family; they also owned the Porter Stores public house in Cross Street where Lloyds Bank now stands. In the 1930s it was Gough's Woollen Mill.

▼ ABERGAVENNY
From near the Station 1893 32591s

Today there are many more large villas here, including those of Fosterville Crescent. Mr Foster, the builder, showed his pride in his work by occupying the largest of the new houses. The stone half way down the other side of the road marked the entry to Mill Lane which led to Mill Street, the main entry road to the town for many centuries.

FRANCIS FRITH'S - ABERGAVENNY

AROUND ABERGAVENNY

ABERGAVENNY
Linda Vista Gardens
c1965 A9131

The landscaping of these gardens was only completed in 1964, following the purchase of Linda Vista House and gardens by the council in 1960. Many unusual plants and trees had been planted in the gardens by previous owners, the Whitehead family. Linda Vista means 'pretty view' in Spanish, a suitable name as this view to the Blorenge mountain shows.

ABERGAVENNY
The Castle from Usk Bridge c1955 A9034

The castle and the south-eastern approaches to the town present an illusion of island tranquillity, stretching from the wide waters of the Usk through the cattle-filled Castle Meadows to the wooded slopes of the Little Skirrid in the distance.

ABERGAVENNY
The Castle c1955 A9049

The raised site chosen for his castle by the Norman Hamelin de Ballon in the late 11th century can be clearly seen here from Castle Meadows. The remains of the 14th-century lodging tower are to the left. Ballon's motte to the right is topped by a 19th-century hunting lodge, which now houses the town's museum.

▲ **ABERGAVENNY,** *The Castle 1893* 32599

The most infamous event in the castle's history occurred in the hall, situated just behind this outer wall. At Christmas 1175 the Norman lord, William de Braose, invited Seisyll ap Dyfnwal and other Welsh nobles to a banquet. At this time there were hopes of a truce in the intermittent warfare between the Normans and the Welsh. Instead, William callously massacred his guests and provoked acts of revenge.

◀ **ABERGAVENNY**
The Castle Bridge 1914
67677s

Three girls pose on the wooden bridge leading to the ivy-clad south-west towers. The rustic walkway presented visitors with ample opportunities to sit and admire the view, and its width is a reminder, if one was needed, of the thickness of the castle's walls.

▲ **ABERGAVENNY,** *The Castle 1914* 67673

The well tended beds, paths and raised walkways show that the Abergavenny Improvement Commissioners had an early appreciation of the ruined castle's leisure and tourist potential. The circle of stones in the foreground stand on the site of the gorsedd stones for the Abergavenny eisteddfodau, organized in the 19th century by Cymregyddion Y Fenni, the Abergavenny Welsh Society.

AROUND ABERGAVENNY

▼ **ABERGAVENNY**
The Castle 1914 67675s

Two of the girls have come down from the bridge and are inspecting the ruined south-west towers. Built around 1300, at the same time as the town walls, the polygonal towers would have provided four floors linked by a spiral staircase. These would have included the lord's apartment, a guard room and a storage area in the basement.

▼ **ABERGAVENNY**
The Castle 1914 67678s

The trees which conceal the south-west towers have now been removed. The steps too were taken out in the 1980s. Here they lead up the motte to the Castle House, which now houses the town's museum.

FRANCIS FRITH'S - ABERGAVENNY

▼ ABERGAVENNY
The Museum c1960 A9126

The buildings now house the town's museum. The museum was opened by Lord Raglan in July 1959, and its first curator was Duggan Thacker. It was extended with the refurbishment of the keep in 1988–1990. The post-war tennis courts on the left are no longer there, and the grounds are now the venue for events such as open-air dramas and historical re-enactments.

▷ ABERGAVENNY
The Castle House 1914 67676s

Standing like a keep, this building was a weekend residence and hunting lodge for the Marquis of Abergavenny; it was built by his steward Mr Baker Gabb between 1815 and 1825. From the late 19th century, after the Marquess had bought Nevill Court, the lodge was leased to tenants, who supplied refreshments to visitors.

AROUND ABERGAVENNY

◀ **ABERGAVENNY**
St Mary's Church
c1960 A9125

After Henry VIII's dissolution of the monasteries in 1542, the Priory Chapel became St Mary's Parish Church. The wide porch and twin gabled west front were part of Thomas Nicholson's restoration of 1881-82. The more recent road sign was no doubt meant to ensure free access to the church for weddings and funerals.

▶ **ABERGAVENNY,** *The Church and the Priory 1898* 41681s

In the late 11th century, a Benedictine priory was founded by Hamelin de Ballon—a conquering Norman lord needed the legitimacy of the church's support. Little of the original priory has survived, but parts of it may have been used when Priory House in the foreground was built in around 1700. A large rambling building, it was demolished in 1952.

FRANCIS FRITH'S - ABERGAVENNY

AROUND ABERGAVENNY

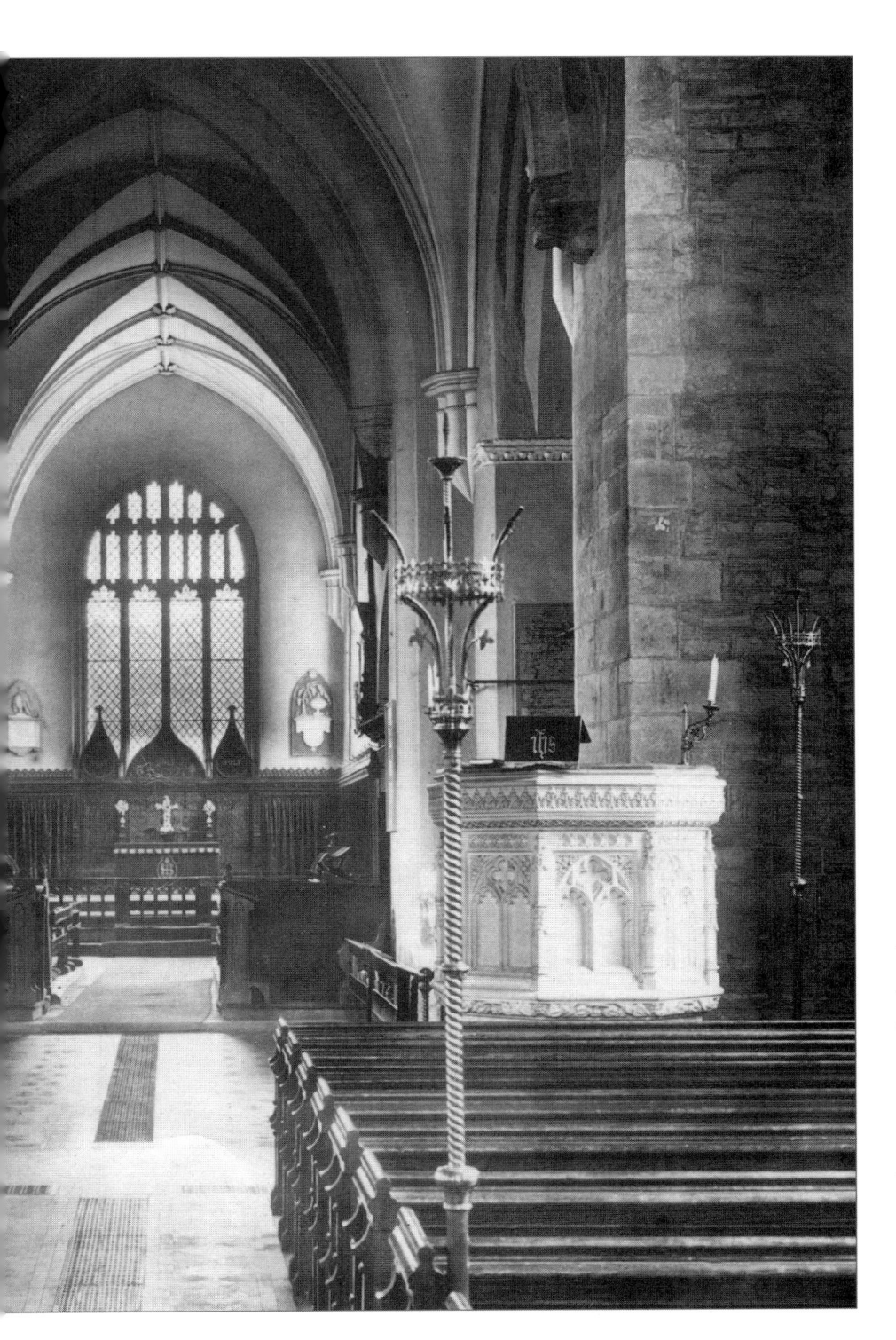

ABERGAVENNY
The Church, the Interior 1898 41775

At the east end of the nave aisle and on each side of the chancel arch are large brass posts with decorated candle holders, five in all. To the right of the nearest one is the staff or wand of the Vicar's Warden—these staffs are usually to be found next to the warden's seat. The nave had been almost completely rebuilt in 1882 and 1896.

FRANCIS FRITH'S - ABERGAVENNY

▼ **ABERGAVENNY,** *St Mary's Church, the Interior 1898* 41678

Beyond the nave and the crossing is the medieval choir and sanctuary, the oldest part of the church, dating from the 12th to the 14th century. It is crowned by an 18th-century vaulted ceiling. The plain east window was to be replaced in 1922 by the colourful stained glass of a memorial window to Brigadier Barker, who was killed in action in the First World War.

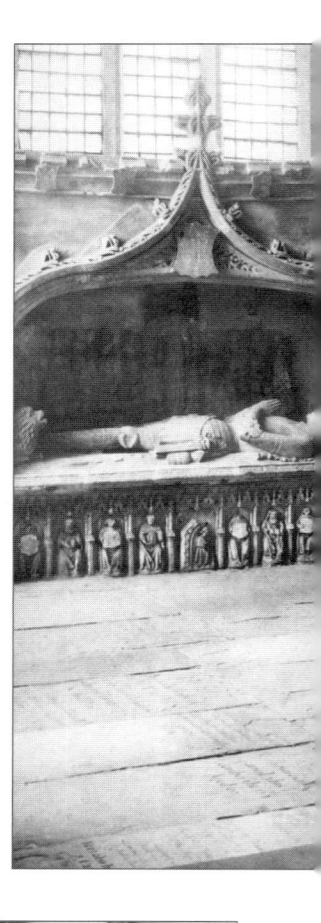

▶ **ABERGAVENNY**
St Mary's Church, the Lewis Chapel 1898 41679s

This chapel takes its name from Dr David Lewis, the son of a vicar of Abergavenny, who became the first principal of Jesus College, Oxford. His tomb is on the left. The Victorian altar and rails have been moved, and the chapel is now home to the Abergavenny Tapestry Group, whose daily stitching will produce a wool on canvas depiction of 1000 years of local history. When completed, it will be displayed in the newly restored tithe barn.

AROUND ABERGAVENNY

◄ **ABERGAVENNY**
St Mary's Church, the Herbert Chapel 1898
41680

In the 15th and 16th centuries, the Herbert family prospered in their family home at Raglan Castle. Three members of the family are buried in this chapel in three magnificent alabaster tombs. In the centre is the tomb of Sir William ap Thomas and his wife Gwladys. In the foreground is the tomb of their son Sir Richard Herbert of Coldbrook and his wife Margaret. Another son, also Sir William, took the name Herbert and was thought to be the most powerful man in Wales from 1465 until his death in 1469. This Sir William was not buried at St Mary's but at Tintern Abbey. The third Herbert tomb in this chapel (to the left) is the elaborate arched tomb of Sir William Herbert's natural son Sir Richard Herbert of Ewyas.

► **ABERGAVENNY**
The Church, the Interior of the Herbert Chapel 1893
32501s

The seven main monuments in the chapel were restored between 1994 and 1998 by an expert team led by Michael Eastham. The reclining oak figure of Jesse in the background has been moved to the north transept to give it more prominence. Originally part of a family tree which showed Christ's ancestry, it is the only wooden sculpture of its kind in Britain.

FRANCIS FRITH'S - ABERGAVENNY

◀ ABERGAVENNY, General View
c1955 A9017

The Town Hall and the Market Hall stand out at the centre; the large building to the right of the Market Hall is Samuel H Facey & Son's brewery, which opened in 1862. In the foreground it is the gentle curve of Monk Street with its buildings of varying sizes, shapes and colours which captures our attention. Even here the developers are busy: the cleared space beyond Laburnum Cottage is soon to be increased in size with the removal of Nos 50 and 51 Cross Street, opposite the Angel Hotel, at the junction with Cross Street.

▲ ABERGAVENNY
From the Church 1898 41667s

This view from St Mary's tower has Monk Street in the foreground. Centre left is the Bethany Baptist Church, which opened in 1827 when 30 members left the Frogmore Street Church. It closed in the 1990s, and has since had a number of uses, including those of furniture showroom and museum of childhood. To the right is the mart, but without the familiar stock pens of today.

FRANCIS FRITH'S - ABERGAVENNY

AROUND ABERGAVENNY

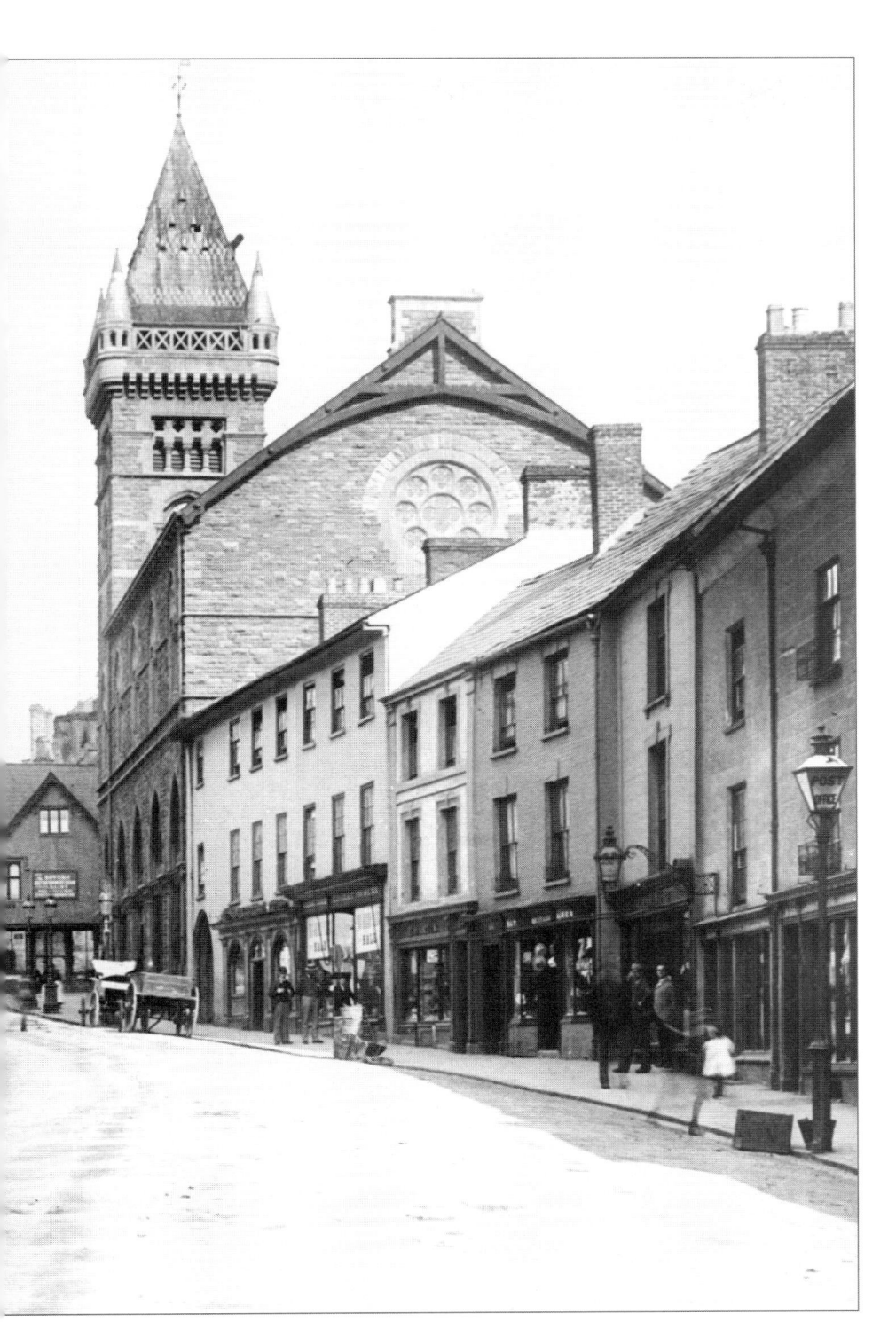

ABERGAVENNY
Cross Street 1893 32596

We can see the letters of part of the surname of the owner, John Prichard, above the entrance to the Angel Hotel on the left. Two doors up there are postcards outside the stationer, bookseller and Athenaeum Library of Evans Harrison. The lamp post on the right marks the site of the town's first post office of 1835. Rising in the centre, the clock tower of the Town Hall of 1870 is a highly visible symbol of civic pride.

FRANCIS FRITH'S - ABERGAVENNY

AROUND ABERGAVENNY

ABERGAVENNY
Cross Street 1898 41675

Postcards can still be seen two doors up from the Angel Hotel, but the store was now owned by C J Fricker. Behind the post office lamp on the right the tall new Lloyds Bank building has altered the roof line. Outside the second store from the right, the Fancy Repository of C H Beddoe, there is a display of baskets.

FRANCIS FRITH'S - ABERGAVENNY

▶ **ABERGAVENNY**
Cross Street 1914 67667

On the left is the sombre but reassuringly secure frontage of the Capital and Counties Bank. The gradual increase in motorized traffic may account for the presence of a policeman at the junction with Monk Street. On that corner, Saunders & Co boldly advertise their agricultural services.

◀ **ABERGAVENNY**
Cross Street c1965
A9136

The new W H Smith building, near left, had replaced the bank since 1926. On the other side of the road the Great George has its familiar and rather curious two-sided sign—it has George Bernard Shaw and George Washington on it. On the opposite corner of Monk Street the agricultural merchants has gone, to be replaced by the new South Wales Electricity Board building.

AROUND ABERGAVENNY

▲ **ABERGAVENNY,** *Frogmore Street c1955* A9075

Frogmore Street begins near the bank on the right, site of the medieval north gate. The pedestrians walking towards the camera are heading for the High Street and, no doubt, the market. E H Hodges, the hairdresser and tobacconist, advertise their wares on their wall and they also sold leather goods and gifts. On the left, another hair stylist is sandwiched between George Oliver's footwear shop and Johnson's dyers and cleaner's.

◄ **ABERGAVENNY**
Frogmore Street c1955
A9077

The road is widening as we look back towards the High Street. Owen the pharmacist was at No 61 (right) until 1958, next door to the King David Inn, which was to close in 1973. Ruther's the fishmonger and grocer's opposite dated from First World War days. The car about to turn left would find today's one-way system against him.

FRANCIS FRITH'S - ABERGAVENNY

▼ **ABERGAVENNY**
Frogmore Street 1914 67669

The White Horse Hotel, right foreground, advertises its select bowling saloon. The horse of the sign seems to be emerging from White Horse Lane just beyond the hotel. The sign on Brown & Seymour's shop beyond reads 'smoke Musketeer tobacco'. At No 17 next door, David Mansfield Scott was a confectioner and mineral water manufacturer; his business operated beside that of Miss Kennington, 'Fancy Draper & Milliner'. The bicycles parked outside the bank on the left might well have been bought at the Cycle & Sports Depot farther down the street. Thoughts of war seem far away in this peaceful, unhurried scene.

▶ **ABERGAVENNY**
Frogmore Street 1893 32597s

A solitary horse and cart is the only traffic at this wide and usually busy junction. To its right stands the cathedral-like front of the Baptist church, built by George Morgan in 1877 at a cost of £4200. The huge wheel window over the double porch is flanked by twin towers. On the extreme right is part of Eastmans Ltd the butcher's, which remained there until 1956.

AROUND ABERGAVENNY

◀ **ABERGAVENNY**
Frogmore Street
c1955 A9076

The Frogmore Café (left) offered busy shoppers a break until 1969, when it was taken over by Sketchleys the cleaners. Barclays Bank, next door, still operates in what has been banking premises for over 120 years. On the right, next to the last parked vehicle, was the town's main post office before the current one was built in St John's Square.

▶ **ABERGAVENNY**
The Monument and the
Baptist Chapel c1965 A9137

At the centre of the junction is the fine war memorial cenotaph designed by Gilbert Ledward in October 1921 and unveiled by Lord Treowen, Lord Lieutenant of the county. A Tesco supermarket now stands on the right where Morgan & Co and M H Maxwell's tobacconist and confectionery businesses can be seen in this photograph. Behind the mini-van on the left, the Butchers Arms had replaced a much older half-timbered building damaged extensively by fire in 1939.

ABERGAVENNY
The Deri from Bailey Park c1960 A9086

The park is the home of Abergavenny Rugby Football Club, and their grandstand can be seen in the middle distance. Much in demand for sporting events, the park is also the venue for steam rallies, shire horse shows and a variety of fundraising events. It is named after Crawshay Bailey, who leased it from 1884 and made an agreement with the Abergavenny Improvement Commissioners to 'empark' it.

ABERGAVENNY, *The River Usk and the Sugar Loaf 1898* 41672

In this idyllic scene much loved by artists and photographers, the River Usk wends its way through wooded banks away from Abergavenny and flows on to join the Severn beyond Newport.

AROUND ABERGAVENNY

ABERGAVENNY
The Little Skirrid and the River Usk
1893 32590

To the Romans the river was Isca, 'a river renowned for its fish'. Certainly it is much loved by fishermen. The river has also been a popular play area for local children, as this late Victorian scene shows. Beyond the town, in the background, is the Little Skirrid mountain, the top of which is not quite as wooded as it is today.

LLANELLEN, *The Church 1898* 41686
At St Helen's Church the corbelled, pinnacled and crocketed tower stands out in more ways than one: it seems curiously at odds, in size and style, with the rest of the church. The projection of the nave walls beyond the wall of the chancel would, as in many churches, have housed the rood-stair in the past.

FRANCIS FRITH'S - ABERGAVENNY

AROUND ABERGAVENNY

LLANOVER
The Church 1898 41690

Llanover is the village where Augusta Waddington, Lady Llanover, made it her mission to revive Welsh language and culture. An English woman, she was a prime mover in the Cymreigyddion, the Abergavenny Welsh Society, formed in 1833. She is buried with her husband Sir Benjamin Hall (after whom Big Ben was named) in Llanover churchyard, to the left of the path. The inscriptions on the large family tomb are, appropriately, bilingual. Nearby are the graves of the Welsh-speaking servants whom Lady Llanover had employed. Their command of the Welsh language had been a prerequisite for their employment.

FRANCIS FRITH'S - ABERGAVENNY

▶ **HOLY MOUNTAIN**
From the Main Road c1955 A9026

Mardy village in 1955 had far less housing than it does today. The semi-detached houses on the left of this picture were the only buildings at that date. The district nurse and midwife Mrs Rowlandson lived in one of them for many years. The houses are now surrounded by the new Croesonnen Park estate, which was begun in 1965. In 1955 the land to the left of the road was part of Chandler's market garden.

◀ **LLANTILIO PERTHOLEY**
The Church and the Skirrid c1960 L579116

The early 14th-century tower of St Teilo's, Llantilio Pertholey stands squarely among the surrounding trees. It is believed that there has been a place of worship on this site since the early 6th century. Beyond it stands the Holy Mountain, Skirrid Fawr, on the summit of which there was once a Roman Catholic chapel dedicated to St Michael.

AROUND ABERGAVENNY

▲ **MARDY,** *The Village c1965* M282002

Since this picture was taken, the 'village' has undergone further housing developments which mean that it has become a suburb of Abergavenny. Extra road traffic has also made the road outside the busy village stores and post office (just to the left of the car) a frequent bottleneck.

LLANTHONY, *The Priory from the North West 1893* 32614

The tranquillity of the Vale of Ewyas and its surrounding hills must have appealed to the Augustinian monks who founded a church here in 1108, possibly on a site where St David, the patron saint of Wales, had lived centuries earlier. Its Welsh name is Llanddewi Nant Honddu, meaning 'the church of St David on the Honddu brook'. The priory itself, built at various times between 1180 and 1230, is in ruins, yet its magnificent setting remains a place for peaceful contemplation. It is a special place. The poet Walter Savage Landor owned the abbey ruins in the early 19th century, and wrote of Llanthony:

'I loved thee by thy streams of yore,

By distant streams I love thee more.'

FRANCIS FRITH'S - ABERGAVENNY

▼ **LLANTHONY,** *The Abbey Hotel 1893* 32617

A mountain track from Longtown was known as 'rhiw cwrw' because it brought beer (cwrw) to the monks. Today's visitors can repair to the bar in the basement of the hotel, which occupies part of the west range of the abbey. Its roof probably dates from the late 18th century, but the steeper pitch of an earlier medieval roof can be seen in the tower wall behind it.

▶ **LLANTHONY**
The Post Office c1955
L80017

The post-box is still on the side of the house, but the post office closed on 8 July 1969. The last person to draw his pension there on 4 July was W J Lewis, a farmer. From then on he was faced with a journey to Llanfihangel Crucorney Post Office. Mrs Powell, the Llanthony postmistress, had a strawberries and cream party to mark the closure.

AROUND ABERGAVENNY

◀ **BRYNMAWR**
Heads of the Valleys Road c1960 B730095

The A465 road on its way westwards from Abergavenny links several South Wales valleys. The stretch from Abergavenny to Ebbw Vale rises at its highest point to 1350ft. Here the 3-lane road winds steeply through the Clydach Gorge towards Brynmawr. Currently it is being widened to make it a dual carriageway.

▶ **BRYNMAWR**
The Market Square c1955
B730071

The war memorial (centre left) commemorates the Royal Welsh Fusiliers of two World Wars so that 'their names will live for evermore'. It is still at the heart of the town, but now it has a black metal surround erected by the Town Council. The Market Hall cinema, showing 'Room at The Top' at the time of this photograph, still operates, though the central window below its clock has gone. The Café Royal (to the left of the war memorial) is now the Homestead Café, and the large New Griffin Hotel, behind it, is now empty and awaiting refurbishment.

FRANCIS FRITH'S - ABERGAVENNY

AROUND ABERGAVENNY

BRYNMAWR
Beaufort Street c1955
B730047

This is the busy main street of the town. Lyndon Sims' well-advertised record shop (note the HMV banner, left) is now a beautician's. His two neighbours nearer the camera were Caleb the greengrocer's (with the delivery bike outside) and an electricity shop. Opposite them, Briggs Stores is now the post office, and Cash & Co beyond is now a kebab shop.

BRYNMAWR
Beaufort Street c1955
B730048

Hodges Garage (in the distance, behind the bus entering Market Square) has since been demolished, and the Castle Hotel (by the street lamp on the right) has also closed. While some bay windows have survived, all the balconies in the street have gone. Eastmans the butcher's (right) and Weeks the butcher's opposite have closed, but Davies, wallpaper and paints (beside Eastmans), has moved to premises further up the street.

BRYNMAWR, *The Semtex Factory c1960* B730103

This rubber factory was built between 1947 and 1953; it was thought to be a visionary building, not least for its roof made up of nine rectangular domes with windows on each of their sides. It is a sad fact that the site became derelict after the factory shut in the early 1980s. Despite a campaign to preserve it, the last phase of its demolition began in 2001.

AROUND ABERGAVENNY

BRYNMAWR, *Llanelly Hill c1960* B730081

The road to Brynmawr winds around the hillside from the village of Gellifelyn, on the right. Near some cottages below the summit of Pen Cyrn mountain, it is just possible to make out the flat ridge on which the former Llangattock tramroad was built from the Nantyglo Ironworks to Llangattock. It is now a cycleway.

FRANCIS FRITH'S - ABERGAVENNY

▼ **BLAENAVON,** *The Eastern Valley c1955* B672009

Standing at the head of the Eastern Valley, in an industrially ravaged landscape, Blaenavon was declared a World Heritage Site in 2000. Amid the trees on the slopes of Coity mountain is the Varteg Cemetery (right). The Rifleman's Arms is the large white building centre right. White House cottage to its right, at the end of Bunker's Row, has now been demolished.

▶ **BLAENAVON**
General View c1955
B672007

On the right is St Peter's, the parish church of Blaenavon, built by the ironmasters Hopkins and Hill in 1805. Almost everything in the church—the pillars, the window frames, the font and the tombs - is made of Blaenavon iron. The church with the central rose window and tower (left) is the Park Street Methodist church, built in 1885–86. To the left of it is the church school, which was well endowed by Miss Sarah Hopkins in 1816.

BLAENAVON
The Workmen's Institute and the Town Clock c1955
B672003

The grand scale and decorated gables of the Institute are a visible reminder of a wealthier town; here the iron-works acted as a magnet which drew workers in huge numbers. Its hall could seat 1500, and the 'stute' was a centre of social life in the town. The war memorial was erected in 1931 from a design by R L Edmunds of Blaenavon.

BLAENAVON
Broad Street c1955
B672001

This street was once called Heol-y-Nant (Brook Street) from the brook which ran through Blaenavon. In the days of the Depression, weekend shoppers thronged it until late at night in their search for bargains, especially food. Briggs's men's wear shop (left) has now closed, ending the firm's involvement in the town from the late 19th century. The Forge Hammer beyond advertises Ansells beer; the pub was to close in 1956.

FRANCIS FRITH'S - ABERGAVENNY

AROUND ABERGAVENNY

BLAENAVON
Broad Street c1955
B672014

We are looking down the street in the opposite direction to photograph B672001, with the Forge Hammer now on the right. Just beyond it on the left is the English Baptist chapel of 1888, now the Evangelical church. There has been a chapel on this site since 1844, and the Baptist tradition has always been strong in the Blaenavon area.

BLAENAVON, *The Memorial to Gilchrist Thomas c1960* B672004

Originally unveiled at Forgeside in 1960, this obelisk in memory of Sidney Gilchrist Thomas is now at the Blaenavon ironworks. The bronze head on the statue was designed and cast by the sculptor Fred Mancini. Thomas and his cousin Percy Carlyle Gilchrist, more famous abroad than in this country, were responsible in 1878-79 for a process which eliminated phosphorus in steel production.

AROUND ABERGAVENNY

◄ CLYDACH
The Wells 1893 32605

This looks like a day out for the men, boys and one woman in the picture. They have chosen a lovely spot at the bottom of Clydach Vale. Its old name was Cwm Pwca (Puck's valley); local legend has it that Shakespeare knew a family in Aberclydach, and wrote 'A Midsummer Night's Dream' here.

◄ *Detail of 32605*

FRANCIS FRITH'S - ABERGAVENNY

CLYDACH
The Lower Fall 1893
32603

The Clydach River is a tributary of the Usk, and joins it between Abergavenny and Crickhowell. Here, about a mile below Devil's Bridge, the river's waters fall rapidly as they travel down the narrow and steep-sided Clydach Valley to the Usk.

LLANFOIST, *The Boathouse on the Canal 1893* 32598

This wharf on the lower slopes of the Blorenge is one of the most photographed places on the Brecknock & Abergavenny Canal. Originally a warehouse, the boathouse behind the trees is now the base of a boat hire company. The steep incline of Hill's tramroad ended just beyond it, and the tramroad continued behind the white wharfinger's cottage before crossing the canal.

AROUND ABERGAVENNY

◢ ABERGAVENNY
From the Canal 1893 32587

Here, from the Brecknock & Abergavenny Canal of 1812, Abergavenny can be seen in the distance. Between the new cemetery in the centre and the allotments and houses to the right, the Merthyr, Tredegar and Abergavenny railway line, opened in 1862, begins its climb of 1000ft to Brynmawr, a mere eight miles away.

◂ *Detail of 32587*

FRANCIS FRITH'S - ABERGAVENNY

▶ **GOVILON**
*The Drawbridge
1936* 87840

Built originally as a drawbridge, Canal Bridge 100 gives access to the Llanwenarth House Hotel. The date 1960 is inscribed on the side of the bridge, which is now a fixed bridge with rolled steel joists and a wooden deck. The car approaching the bridge is a 1932 Austin 7, which had its petrol tank under the bonnet. Models from 1934 onwards had the tank under the back of the car.

◀ **GILWERN**
*The Main Road
c1955* G246002

The Premier Wireless Stores on the right is now Dean's TV Services. It and Hatherleigh next door were built as one building in 1903. Opposite, Craven A cigarettes were on sale at Ron James's general stores, now a private residence. Further down on the left is the road junction for Llangattock and Crickhowell just before the white building, the Beaufort Arms.

AROUND ABERGAVENNY

▲ **GILWERN,** *The Canal c1955* G246004

The landlords of the Bridgend Inn, the rear of which is on the left, were George and Betty Dobson, and the busy boat hire business operating from the hut further down the towpath was owned by a Mr Price. One of the lads who worked for him by bailing out his boats was Graham Jones, who is the current landlord at the Bridgend Inn.

◀ **GILWERN**
The Canal c1955
G246007

Just along the canal from Bridge 104, the boat is emerging from a turning point in the canal basin. The bank to the right, where the car is parked, now houses a boat hire firm, Castle Narrowboats. Above the trees and below the houses in the centre, the busy Heads of the Valleys road passes very close to the canal.

FRANCIS FRITH'S - ABERGAVENNY

▼ **LLANWENARTH CITRA,** *The Church 1898* 41683

St Peter's stands in meadows beside the Usk, to the left of the A40 and just beyond the western outskirts of Abergavenny. The parish of Llanwenarth was divided into two parts, Llanwenarth Citra and Llanwenarth Ultra, by the River Usk. St Peter's Church was in Llanwenarth Citra. The two Llanwenarths were joined by a rope ferry, which closed down in 1951. From the churchyard there is a magnificent view of the Blorenge mountain. The medieval cross near the tree on the left is still a broken remnant at this date. It was restored 'in grateful memory of all who served and those who fell in the War for right and freedom 1914-1919', and it also remembers those who served and fell in the Second World War.

▶ **LLANWENARTH CITRA**
The Church, the Interior 1898 41684

St Peter's was restored extensively in the 19th century. Though there are a number of candles on the pulpit and in the chandelier suspended from the ceiling, it is likely that oil lamps would also have been used at this time.

72

AROUND ABERGAVENNY

◀ **CRICKHOWELL**
The View from the Dardy c1955
C188083

Here the expanding village can be seen from the Llangattock side of the Usk. To the left, a diagonal road of houses rises en route to Llanbedr. In the centre in the background is the Sugar Loaf.

▶ **CRICKHOWELL**
The Bridge 1893
32606

The long bridge over the wide Usk river separates Crickhowell from the neighbouring village of Llangattock. It is a curious fact that the side shown in the picture has thirteen arches, whilst the other side has one fewer. In the centre the long white building is the 16th-century Bridge End Inn, at the junction of New Road and Bridge Street.

FRANCIS FRITH'S - ABERGAVENNY

AROUND ABERGAVENNY

CRICKHOWELL
The Bridge 1931
C188004

In the absence of a pavement, the two men in the centre have found a safe spot whilst they put the world to rights. Behind them, New Road rises to the village centre and to the A40 road to Brecon and Abergavenny. At the top of the hill stands the steeple of the 14th-century parish church of St Edmund. The flat-topped hill above the tall tree on the left is Table Mountain or Crug Hywel, from which the village gets its name.

FRANCIS FRITH'S - ABERGAVENNY

CRICKHOWELL
High Street 1898 41695

Now the Dragon Hotel, the Dragon Inn (left) first opened in 1740. Its licensee in 1898 was Elizabeth Davies. Outside it stands a row of watering cans on a sheet of corrugated iron balanced between two barrels. Farther along are more barrels and boxes. Outside the lower building next door, now a private residence, is a display of spades. On the other side of the road is a lamp post advertising the post office. Today the post office is gone, but a modern, larger lamp of similar style is attached to the wall of Carlton House, No 25. The ivy-clad house on the right, Latham House, retains its railings but has lost the ivy.

FRANCIS FRITH'S - ABERGAVENNY

▼ **CRICKHOWELL,** *Market Square and High Street 1951* C188026

The monument in Market Square is inscribed: 'In memory of Henry John Lucas M D. Born July 3rd 1804 Died December 29th 1873'. To the right, Williams & Wilde's baker's shop is next door to the awnings of Isaacs the greengrocer's.

▶ **CRICKHOWELL**
The Market Place 1931
C188003

The bus advertising E A Beveridge & Co and the cars are of an earlier vintage, but the buildings still look much the same. Centre left stands the Bear Hotel, a lovely old coaching inn dating back to 1432. The shop next door to it sold fishing tackle—fishing is one of the area's most popular pastimes. The public house on the right, the Corn Exchange, advertises stabling.

AROUND ABERGAVENNY

◀ **CRICKHOWELL**
High Street c1965
C188194

The columns on the left are on the front of the Market Hall below the old court house. Next door to the Bear Hotel is Kirkland's the chemist's. Evans's tobacconist's and sweet shop next to the chemist's also did removals, and the tall end building was a café. The Corn Exchange pub on the right advertises Hancocks Ales, and the Corona lemonade crates on the lorry offer an alcohol-free alternative.

▶ **CRICKHOWELL**
The Castle 1951
C188029

Little remains of Robert de Turbeville's early 12th-century motte and bailey castle. Its stone successor was built in 1272 by Sir Grimbauld Pauncefote. This was ruined in 1403 during Owain Glyndwr's revolt, and only the motte and a couple of towers remain. The tower has been further reduced since 1951 to provide stone for garden walls.

FRANCIS FRITH'S - ABERGAVENNY

AROUND ABERGAVENNY

LLANVETHERINE
The Village c1950
L386002

On the right is Waterloo Cottage, which until the mid 1970s was the post office and village shop. The Cwmera Baptist church on the left was built in 1868, and the shed next to its graveyard was once used to stable the horses of visiting preachers.

▶ LLANVETHERINE
The Church c1950
L386003

A most interesting architectural feature of the church of St James the Elder at Llanvetherine is the tower. The top battlemented section overhangs the corbel table, lending it the appearance of a recently completed jigsaw.

◀ LLANVETHERINE
White Castle c1950
L386001

Edward I was renowned for his military strongholds, especially in North Wales. In 1254, as a young prince, he was granted the trilateral castles of White Castle, Grosmont and Skenfrith. Probably he was responsible for this twin-towered gatehouse, which in the 1260s became the new entrance to the castle via a drawbridge over the deep moat.

▲ **LLANVETHERINE,** *White Castle c1950* L386004

It is not difficult to see why the grassy inner ward of this formidable castle became one of the picnic destinations of Rudolf Hess. The Nazi Deputy Fuhrer was a prisoner at Maindiff Court Hospital from June 1942 to October 1945. On his excursions with his guards he became a familiar figure to local people.

◀ **RAGLAN**
The Castle 1893 32533

The Pitched Stone Court at Raglan took its name from the pitching or cobbling of its surface. The ivy-clad walls retain a richness of style, not least in the transomed and mullioned oriel window of the hall on the right. A library in the battlemented rear gatehouse range once held a priceless collection of Welsh manuscripts and books, wantonly destroyed by Oliver Cromwell's troops.

RAGLAN, *The Castle from The Moat 1893* 32531

The machicolated heights of William Herbert's gatehouse and closet towers look down on the moat which surrounds the famous Yellow Tower, the work of his father William ap Thomas. King Henry VII spent some of his childhood at Raglan, where the two Williams had transformed a fortified rural manor into a castle fit for a future king.

AROUND ABERGAVENNY

▲ **RAGLAN**
The Village 1906 54520

The road is Station Road, which today leads to the golf course. The church tower continues to dominate this scene, but the village has grown a lot in the last century, with new schools, new housing and a new surgery.

Detail of 54520

FRANCIS FRITH'S - ABERGAVENNY

AROUND ABERGAVENNY

RAGLAN
High Street 1914 67687

There is documentary evidence that the Ship Inn on the left dates from at least 1600, and its cobbled courtyard remains today thanks to a preservation order. Opposite it, Davies & Jones's store seems to be a meeting-point for the local boys and their bicycles. As the High Street disappears in the distance it becomes the Monmouth Road.

FRANCIS FRITH'S - ABERGAVENNY

RAGLAN
The Church c1955
R3036

A little church with a large tower, it is dedicated to St Cadoc, but it is said to have been founded by St David. The 15th-century tower has four pinnacles and large gargoyles leaning out over its panelled buttresses. The Somerset chapel on the left is the last resting place of several of the Earls of Worcester, masters of Raglan Castle.

RAGLAN, *Castle Street 1914* 67684

The lad may be returning from the castle, which could be approached on this road at that time. The four houses on the right, built in 1817, are now private residences. Two of them still have large windows by their doors to remind us that they used to be the corner stores and Jones's Refreshment Rooms. Most of the trees remain, but they have been severely cut back.

INDEX

Abergavenny
Baptist Chapel 49
Black Mountains 19
The Blorenge 22, 24, 25
The Bridge 23
The Bus Depot 26
The Castle 30-33
The Castle House 34
Cross Street 42-46
The Deri 50
Frogmore Street 47-49
The Gavenny 27
General View 40-41
Holy Mountain 19
Linda Vista Gardens 29
Monmouth Road 25
The Monument 49
The Museum 34
The River Usk 23, 50-51
St Mary's Church 26, 34-39
The Sugar Loaf 16–18, 20-21, 50

Surrounding Area
Blaenavon 62–63, 64–65, 66
Brynmawr 56–57, 58–59, 60, 61
Clydach 67, 68
Crickhowell 72–73, 74–75, 76–77, 78–79
Gilwern 70, 71
Govilon 70–7
Holy Mountain 54–55
Llanellen 51
Llanfoist 68
Llanover 52–53
Llanthony 55, 56
Llantilio Pertholey 54
Llanvetherine 80–81, 82–83
Llanwenarth Citra 72
Mardy 55
Raglan 83, 84, 85, 86–87, 88,

Acknowledgements

Thanks should go to the following people:

Louis Bannon for his permission to use Frith's postcards A9017, A9051, A9075, and A9077, from his extensive collection. Frank Olding for his knowledge of Blaenau Gwent and Abergavenny. Rachael Rogers and the staff at Abergavenny Museum. The volunteers who run Blaenavon and Brynmawr Museums. The staff at Newport Library. Irena Morgan, the committee and members of the Abergavenny Local History Society. Gareth Davies of g-media.co.uk for the map. The numerous locals who shared their recollections of their area.

FURTHER READING LIST

Abergavenny Local History Society
    Abergavenny Street Survey 1979-1984 (Reference only.)

Bannon, Louis
    Remember Abergavenny Vol 1, Old Bakehouse Publications, 1995

Barber, Chris
    Exploring Blaenavon Industrial Landscape World Heritage Site, Blorenge Books, 2002

Davies, Canon E T
    The Place Names of Gwent, The Starling Press 1982

Davies, Richard
    A Church, Two Chapels and a School, 1999
    And So To School, 2000

Davies, Richard (Ed)
    A Town Remembers: Memories of Wartime Abergavenny 1939-1945, Abergavenny Local History Society, 2nd edn, 2003

Howell, Raymond
    A History of Gwent, Gomer Press, 1992

Jones, Gwyn (with illustrations by Michael Blackmore)
    A Walk around Abergavenny, 1990
    Prehistoric Abergavenny
    Roman Abergavenny, 1982
    Medieval Town and Market of Abergavenny
    Medieval Abergavenny, 1984

Morgan, I M
    Abergavenny Past & Present, Sutton Publishing, 2003

Newman, John
    The Buildings of Wales Gwent/Monmouthshire (Pevsner Architectural Guides), Penguin Books University of Wales Press 2000

Olding, Frank
    Vanished Abergavenny-Y Fenni Ddiflanedig, Sutton Publishing, 1994

Stevens, R Alan
    Brecknock & Abergavenny and Monmouthshire Canals, Goose and Son, 1974

Tucker, Anna
    Abergavenny in Old Photographs, Abergavenny Museum

Also well worth a visit is the Abergavenny Local History Society website:
    www.abergavennyhistory.co.uk

NAMES OF SUBSCRIBERS

The following people have kindly supported this book by subscribing to copies before publication.

Abergavenny Chronicle

Bob, Cheryl & Peter Andrews

Mrs M A S Beckett, Abergavenny

Sheila Bevan

Dr A F Bissell & Mrs E Bissell

Hazel Buchanan, Abergavenny

M & A Chamberlain, Crickhowell

Dr & Mrs Coldrey, Abergavenny

Mr M & Mrs P A Cox, Abergavenny

Mrs G Davies, Abergavenny

Mr P & Mrs E J Duckworth

Peter & Anne Davis

P F Farrar

The Foster Family

The Griffiths Family

Maureen Griffiths, Abergavenny

Brenda Mary Hacking of Abergavenny

Pryderi Hughes, Abergavenny

In memory of Irvin Jenkins, Abergavenny

John & Carole Jones

The Jones Family, Abergavenny

Keith & Elizabeth Jones

Michelle Joseph, Blaenavon

John Kerr

R T King, Abergavenny

John & Veronica McIntyre (nee Morgan)

Mr J H G & Mrs E J J Meredith, Hillgrove

Colin Morgan

To Mum on your 70th birthday, love Jane

Peter Nunn

The Poplar Family

Connie Porter & Family

Roger, Jane & Anne Rimner

W J Scrimgeour & R J Scrimgeour

To Eryl Sheers on her 60th birthday

Sonia Skinner & John Skinner

Charles Smith

Wayne Thomas

The Thomas Family, Abergavenny

The Tyler Family

E C G Vater, Abergavenny

The Walker Family, Govilon

Sarah Walker

Mary White, Abergavenny

Les & Sheila Williams, Blaenavon

For Peter Williams, who loved his town

Christopher Wills-Wood

Michael Wills-Wood

Nigel Wills-Wood

Paddy Wills-Wood

FRITH PRODUCTS & SERVICES

Francis Frith would doubtless be pleased to know that the pioneering publishing venture he started in 1860 still continues today. Over a hundred and forty years later, The Francis Frith Collection continues in the same innovative tradition and is now one of the foremost publishers of vintage photographs in the world. Some of the current activities include:

Interior Decoration

Today Frith's photographs can be seen framed and as giant wall murals in thousands of pubs, restaurants, hotels, banks, retail stores and other public buildings throughout the country. In every case they enhance the unique local atmosphere of the places they depict and provide reminders of gentler days in an increasingly busy and frenetic world.

Product Promotions

Frith products are used by many major companies to promote the sales of their own products or to reinforce their own history and heritage. Frith promotions have been used by Hovis bread, Courage beers, Scots Porage Oats, Colman's mustard, Cadbury's foods, Mellow Birds coffee, Dunhill pipe tobacco, Guinness, and Bulmer's Cider.

Genealogy and Family History

As the interest in family history and roots grows world-wide, more and more people are turning to Frith's photographs of Great Britain for images of the towns, villages and streets where their ancestors lived; and, of course, photographs of the churches and chapels where their ancestors were christened, married and buried are an essential part of every genealogy tree and family album.

Frith Products

All Frith photographs are available Framed or just as Mounted Prints and Posters (size 23 x 16 inches). These may be ordered from the address below. From time to time other products - Address Books, Calendars, Table Mats, etc - are available.

The Internet

Already fifty thousand Frith photographs can be viewed and purchased on the internet through the Frith websites and a myriad of partner sites.

For more detailed information on Frith companies and products, look at these sites:

www.francisfrith.co.uk
www.francisfrith.com
(for North American visitors)

See the complete list of Frith Books at:

www.francisfrith.co.uk

This web site is regularly updated with the latest list of publications from the Frith Book Company. If you wish to buy books relating to another part of the country that your local bookshop does not stock, you may purchase on-line.

For further information, trade, or author enquiries please contact us at the address below:
The Francis Frith Collection, Frith's Barn, Teffont, Salisbury, Wiltshire, England SP3 5QP.
Tel: +44 (0)1722 716 376   Fax: +44 (0)1722 716 881   Email: sales@francisfrith.co.uk

See Frith books on the internet at www.francisfrith.co.uk